AF255885

AUSTRALIAN COMMONWEALTH MILITARY FORCES
Lest We Forget

First published 2026
ISBN: 978-0-6458712-4-1

Publisher: Remember When Books
www.rememberwhen-books.com.au

Printed by IngramSpark in Melbourne, Australia

MY FIRST DAWN SERVICE

Written by
Peta Wilson

Illustrated by
Caroline Keys

Remember When Books

"Pop, what was the war like?" I asked him one day.
While out in his garden, he was digging away.
Glancing up from his patch, his eyes start to fade,
he continued to dig with his long-handled spade.

He did not answer, not a word!
Maybe my question went unheard.

"What are you baking?" I asked my Nan.
Secretly hoping to help if I can.
She added the oats, some sugar and butter.
"Do you need the cookie cutter?"

"Today I am making a special treat.
These are the biscuits we LOVE to eat!
We'll bake them 'til they're golden brown."
Nan twists the timer and sets it down.

Chatting away, she opens the door.
"We sent these in tins to the soldiers at war."

I try some mixture straight from the spoon.
"It tastes so good, I hope they're cooked soon."

"We made them for soldiers to lift their low spirits.
You've had them before,
they're Anzac Biscuits!"

Once they're cool, I take a bite.
"They are delicious!" I hug her tight.
She pours some tea from her silver pot
and takes a seat in her usual spot.

"Pop didn't answer when we were outside!"
"What did you ask him?" her eyes growing wide.
"I asked him to tell me about the olden days.
I'm sure he heard me but had nothing to say".

"I'm sure he did hear you, but it's been a long time.
He won't answer questions... not even mine.
It brings up some memories that make him feel sad.
It's not that our questions are wrong or bad.
It's hard to imagine, since we were not there.
Tomorrow, we'll show him how much we care."

Tomorrow I'm going to my first dawn service.
I've not been before, I'm feeling quite nervous.
We go to bed early as we need a big sleep.
I get tucked in tight and start counting sheep.

"Do I have to get up? It's still dark outside!"
Pop's ready to go and brimming with pride.
The weather is fresh, it feels quite cold.
Pop's holding his hat and I see something gold!

Not quite awake, I slide in the car.
Pop whispers gently, "We're not going far!"

"We'll see you later, enjoy your day!"
We give him a kiss and he's on his way.
While we are walking, I notice a crowd.
All of them quiet, sombre and proud.

Nan holds my hand and gives it a squeeze,
that instantly puts me right at ease.

In the distance, I hear the beat of a drum,
a slow, steady sound as the marchers come.
Bagpipes are sounding so soft in the night,
I listen and wait in the pale dawn light.

Then marching feet, beat by beat,
'Til I finally see them come up the street.
They march in their lines with precision and order,
until they stop at the invisible border.

Silence falls and all is still,
no drums or pipes from up the hill.
We stand together, side by side,
so calm, so quiet and full of pride.

A single bugle starts to play,
its gentle notes drift far away.
Nobody moves. Nobody speaks.
Everyone is up out of their seats.

They all stand still, their eyes ahead.
I am so glad I didn't stay in bed.
As we listen, they speak of war.
The brave men and women, we remember them all.

I look up at my Nan, she's got tears in her eyes.
Then warmth hits my face, as the sun starts to rise.

These tears are the memories of loved ones, a friend,
fighting so bravely, right 'til the end.
Sharing some stories from so long ago,
of painful memories they'd rather let go.

They say that years later, it's not any better.
Then someone begins to share an old letter.

It's from a young man, sent to his mum.
He'd just turned eighteen, her only son.
He never returned to the family's land,
nor did he get to become an old man.

The people they speak of, I did not know,
but taking part in this service just goes to show
that while we may not know their names,
we will remember their bravery, all the same.

"Everyone has a part to play.
There is now something we all have to say.
You may not know the words just yet,
but look to the sky, here come the jets!"

This poem we say comes straight from the heart.
We say it together, each playing our part.
Reciting it proudly, year after year,
and I find it always brings me to tears.

Removing their hats like a heavy load.
Everyone starts to recite the ode.

As the flags are strung up, the soldiers salute.
The Last Post plays, a final tribute.

"We remember the fallen who fought for our country,
who sacrificed much, ever so humbly."
The man calls out and they salute once more,
just like they did when they went off to war.

Side by side they gather each year.
To march, remember and shed a tear.

Brave men and women, not knowing their fate.
Who went off to war to stand with their mate.

Now heading towards us, a purposeful stride,
medals displayed on his chest with great pride.

"Poppy!" I shout as he starts to near.
Nan looks at him proudly and wipes a tear.

He gathers me up and hugs me so tight.
I hug him back with all of my might.

I may be small, but I know what to say.
"Thank you for bringing me here today.
I don't need an answer, I just want you to know.
Poppy, you are my hero!"

On the 25th of April, year after year,
you may find yourself also shedding a tear.
Remember those heroes and stand up tall.
The spirit of the Anzac lives in us all.

They shall grow not old, as we that are left grow old;
Age shall not weary them, nor the years condemn.
At the going down of the sun and in the morning.
We will remember them.

Response:
We will remember them
Lest we forget

AUSTRALIAN COMMONWEALTH
MILITARY FORCES

L/Cpl Colin Alexander Abra

In loving memory of my grandfather

NX41291

Lance Corporal
Colin Alexander Abra
2/10 Australian General Hospital
Prisoner of War, Changi, Singapore

Born 7 June 1919
Died 4 August 2002

Loved husband, father, grandfather, great-grandfather and mate.
We remember with pride, love and deep gratitude.

This is my grandfather, Colin Alexander Abra.

He served during the Second World War and was a Prisoner of War.

He and many others showed great bravery, courage and resilience during very difficult times. There was little food or medicine, yet they continued to support one another through long days of labour and illness.

Though the war ended, its memories stayed with him for life.

We also remember the mates who never made it home.

They are never forgotten.

TEACHER AND CAREGIVER NOTE

This story introduces themes of war, remembrance and service in a gentle and age-appropriate way.

Some references may raise questions or emotions for children, particularly those with personal or family connections to military service. Teachers and caregivers are encouraged to guide discussions thoughtfully and to share only as much detail as is suitable for the age, readiness and needs of their students.

This book is intended to support respectful conversations about Anzac Day, bravery and remembrance in a safe and supportive environment.

ABOUT THE AUTHOR

Peta Wilson is an educator and children's author from regional New South Wales. Through her work in schools and her love of storytelling, she creates books that support gentle conversations between children, families and classrooms.

My First Dawn Service was written to help young readers understand the meaning of Anzac Day in a way that feels safe, respectful and connected to family tradition.

AUSTRALIAN
COMMONWEALTH
MILITARY FORCES
Lest We Forget

www.ingramcontent.com/pod-product-compliance
Lightning Source LLC
Chambersburg PA
CBRC102023050726
47602CB00012B/164